WALFORD'S
CROYD(

com

John W. Brown

LOCAL HISTORY REPRINTS

316 GREEN LANE, STREATHAM, LONDON SW16 3AS

Originally printed in 1883-4 by
Cassell and Company Limited
as part of
Greater London
by
Edward Walford M.A.

This edition published in 1993 by
Local History Reprints
316 Green Lane
Streatham
London SW16 3AS

ISBN 1 85699 028 1

INTRODUCTION

Edward Walford was born at Hatfield Place, near Chelmsford, on 3rd February 1823. His family roots were well and truly planted in the Church, his father, the Rev. William Walford, being the Rector of St. Runwald's Church, Colchester, and his mother, Mary Ann Walford, being the daughter of the Rev. Henry Hutton, Rector of Beaumont in Essex, and chaplain of Guy's Hospital.

As befitted a clergyman's son he attended the Church of England school at Hackney, where he was tutored by Edward Churton, later to become Archdeacon of Cleveland. After this he went to Charterhouse, one of England's finest public schools which was then under the headship of Augustus Page Saunders, later to become Dean of Peterborough.

Edward was a gifted scholar, and matriculated from Balliol College, Oxford, in 1841. In 1843 he won the chancellor's prize for latin verse, and graduated B.A. in 1845 and M.A. two years later in 1847.

Not surprisingly, given his family background and education, he was ordained a deacon in 1846, becoming a priest in the following year. His flair for learning continued and he was successful in winning the Denyer theological prize in both 1847 and 1848.

His early career was pursued in the world of education. His first post in 1846 was that of assistant-master at Tonbridge School. This was followed from 1847-1850 by a period as a private tutor when he prepared pupils in both London and Clifton for entry to Oxford.

Edward met his first wife, Mary Holmes, whilst teaching in Clifton in 1847, and by her had a daughter, Mary Louisa. In February 1852 he married for a second time when he took as his bride Julia Talbot, the daughter of Admiral Sir John Talbot.

In the 1850's Walford's career moved more and more towards writing and he had several books published including a "Handbook on the Greek Drama." In June 1858 he became the editor of the "Court Circular," however this was not a successful venture, and a year later he withdrew from the position after losing £500 in the venture.

This early set back did not appear to dampen his enthusiasm, and from 1859 to 1865 he was connected with the periodical "Once a Week," first as sub-editor, and afterwards as editor.

This was followed by a period of almost 30 months as editor of the famous "Gentleman's Magazine" which he left in May 1868 when the publication came under new management.

His editorial duties did not prevent Edward from writing, and he produced a series of biographical and genealogical publications including "Records of the Great and Noble" in 1857, "County Families of Great Britain" in 1860 and "Life of the Prince Consort" in 1861.

His publication of cheap reference works such as "Hardwicke's Shilling Baronetage and Knightage," "Hardwicke's Shilling Peerage," and "Hardwicke's Shilling House of Commons," gained him a reputation as a popular writer of his day.

Walford is best remembered today for his topographical books on London. Following the death of George Thornbury in 1876, Edward continued the major Victorian history of our capital city which Thornbury had started in 1872, completing the last four of the six volumes of "London Old and New" in 1878.

The following year he published a further two volumes on London called "Londoniana."

His trio of major works on London was completed in 1883-4 when he published two volumes entitled "Greater London." This publication adopted the same format as "London Old and New" and dealt with the history of London's rapidly expanding outer suburbs.

Walford divided the history of Croydon into four chapters, the first covering the early history of Croydon and its parish church; the second, the Archbishops' Palace; the third, Whitgift's Hospital and other charities; and the fourth, a general history of Croydon and the surrounding area.

It is from the first chapter that the following pages on Croydon are taken. The text is illustrated with a number of engravings, including a full page view of Croydon from the south-east showing its then rural location, with bundles of wheat stacked up in a nearby field.

Walford's London books drew heavily from the writings of previous historians, none the less it is true to say that the eight volumes of "Old and New London" and "Greater London" provided the standard reference work on the capital for generations of Londoners.

He was the last of the great Victorian writers on London and no history of the metropolis of similar size, style or popular appeal has been published since his volumes. Even today, many books on London quote from his text, which is a fitting testimonial to the value of his work.

Edward died at Ventnor on the Isle of Wight on 20th November 1897.

JOHN W. BROWN

CROYDON - EARLY HISTORY

Situation and Early History - Etymology of Name
Discovery of coins -Historical Associations
The Old and New Churches of St. John the Baptist
Destruction and Rebuilding - Monuments and Epitaphs
Mural Painting in the Church - Register
Dr. William Cleiver and the Highwayman

When we near Croydon, we feel that, however modern its present appearance may be, we are approaching a place once famous as the dwelling of holy men of old, some of whom at all events have gained places in the calendar of the unreformed Church.

Here the names of Lanfranc and Kilwardby and Winchelsea, Courtenay and Chicheley and Arundel, and Warham and Cranmer, sound almost as truly "household words" as at Oxford or Cambridge, at Westminster or Lambeth. The very air here is redolent of churchmanship of the past Saxon type, and our only regret is that we can learn so little about their Anglo-Saxon predecessors.

But, alas! Though Croyland and Malmesbury and Waltham figure there, we can find no reference at all to Croydon in Mr. E. A. Freeman's "Old English History," a book which treats fully of the Saxon times.

The town of Croydon is now the largest in all Surrey, and occupies a pleasant position on the Brighton Road, about ten miles from London. The nucleus of it is a well-built street, about a mile in length, called the High Street. This was in former times nothing more than a bridle way over the fields; but leading over higher ground, and in a more direct course that the way through the old town, by usage it became the principal road, and was at length built upon, and superseded the former highway.

Croydon parish is bounded on the north by Lambeth and Streatham, on the east by Penge, the parishes of Beckenham and West Wickham, in Kent, and that of Addington, in Surrey; on the south by Addington, Sanderstead, and Coulsdon, and on the west by Beddington and Mitcham; it is no less than thirty-six miles in circumference, and the soil is, in different parts of the parish, chalk, gravel, sand, clay, and peat.

Lysons mentions a large chalk-pit about a mile from the town, near the road to Addington, which afforded a large number of fossils; indeed, all the southern side is chalk.

Croydon lies in the opening of a rich and beautiful vale, as Camden observes, "lying under the hills." Speaking generally, those to the east are wooded, those to the west and south-west are mostly open downs.

Domesday Book

The manor of Croydon is thus described in the "Domesday Book" among the lands of the Archbishop of Canterbury :-

> "In the hundred of Waleton (Wallington) Archbishop Lanfranc holds Croindene in demesne.
>
> "In the time of King Edward it was assessed at 80 hides, now at 16 hides and 1 virgate. The arable land amounts to 20 carucates.
>
> "There are in the demesne 4 carucates, and forty-eight villains and twenty-five bordars, with 34 carucates. There is a church, and one mill at 5s., and 8 acres of meadow. The wood yields two hundred swine.
>
> "Of the land belonging to this manor, Restolf holds of the archbishop 7 hides, and Ralph 1 hide; and thence they have £7.8s. rent.
>
> "The whole manor, in the time of King Edward, was valued at £12; now at £27 to the archbishop, and £10 10s to his men."

This manor is said to have been given by William 1 to Archbishop Lanfranc, who is supposed to have founded the archiepiscopal palace, though Robert Kilwardby is the first prelate who is certainly known to have resided at Croydon.

He resigned the metropolitan dignity on being made a cardinal, in 1278, and went to Rome, leaving the castles and mansions belonging to the see in such a dilapidated state, that Archbishop Peckham, his successor, found it necessary to expend 3,000 marks in repairs, though it is uncertain what part of this sum may have been laid out at Croydon.

The manor continued to belong to the see of Canterbury until the troubles of the seventeenth century, when the revenues of the archbishopric were seized by the Parliament. The annual value of the manor, place, and land, was then estimated at £275, exclusive of the timber.

Old Croydon Church in 1785

Croydon is first mentioned in the joint will of Beorhtrie and Ælfswyth dated about 962

The manor-house, or palace, situated near the church, was for several hundred years the occasional residence of the Archbishops of Canterbury, who had attached to it a park and grounds containing 170 acres. These stretched away on to the high ground to the south-east. Of this park the famous Sir William Walworth was keeper in the reign of Richard II. In July, 1573, Archbishop Parker entertained Queen Elizabeth and her whole Court here seven days, and Whitgift received more than one visit from the same princess at this palace.

The Civil War

When the possessions of the see of Caterbury were seized by the Parliament during the civil war with Charles I, Croydon Palace was first leased to the Earl of Nottingham, and afterwards to Sir William Brereton, the famous Parliamentary General, "a notable man, at a thanksgiving dinner," writes a pamphleteer of the time quoted by Lysons, "having terrible long teeth, and a prodigious stomach to turn the archbishop's chapel into a kitchen, and to swallow up that palace and lands at a morsel. After the Restoration this edifice was fitted up, and restored to its former state by archbishop Juxon." We shall treat more fully of the archiepiscopal palace in the next chapter.*

Origins of Name

Croydon is first mentioned in the joint will of Beorhtrie and Ælfswyth, dated about 962. It is there spelt *Crogoene.* "Crog," says Mr. J. Corbet Anderson, in his "Chronicle of Croydon Parish," "was, and still is, the Norse, or Danish, word for crooked, such is expressed in Anglo-Saxon by *crumb,* a totally different word.

"From the Danish came our *crook* and *crooked.* This term accurately describes the locality. It is a *crooked,* or *winding valley,* a reference to the valley which runs in an oblique and serpentine course from Godstone to Croydon.

"The Anglo-Saxon *g* is equivalent to our *y;* and thus the name was pronounced in 962 exactly at it is now, with the substitution only in the final syllable of the letter *o* for the diphthong *œ,* a very common and venial corruption. In any question relating to the meaning of names, the most ancient form of spelling them ought to have great weight.

* See separate booklet in this series on Walford's History of Croydon Palace.

"In the entry in 'Domesday Book' relative to the manor, the Normans spelt its name *Croindene;* hence, Garrow supposed that the term originated in the union of the two Saxon words - *crone*, 'sheep', and *dene*, 'a valley' - sheep-valley.

"Ducarel considered that the name Croydon was derived from the old Norman-French word *cray*, or *craie*, 'chalk,' and the Saxon *dun*, 'a hill,' meaning a town near the chalk-hill; but this surmise is open to the objection that long ere the Norman language could have so prevailed the place was known, as we have seen, almost by its present name."

Croydon is a religious town, for, whether the final syllable be only "town" in disguise, or whether it be derived from the denes, dennes, or dunes, that surround it, the final syllable points to *croix*, a cross, as lying at its origin. It was the town of the cross - the town where the Christian faith was known, professed, and preached; it is to be hoped was practised also.

It was not a military station; not a seat of trade or commerce; but a seat of religion. As such it could not fail to attract to it such converts as were made in the pagan districts that surrounded it; and so in very early days became populous. Mr. M. F. Tupper and Mr. Thorne suggest a more prosaic derivation of the name, viz., *craie*, chalk. As was generally the case with old ecclesiastical towns, the parish is most extensive, being, as we have already seen, no less that thirty-six miles in circuit.

A Curious Discovery

A curious discovery of remains of the old Saxon rule was made at Croydon in June 1862. In the course of constructing the railway from West Croydon to Balham, the excavators found, at about two feet below the surface, what they called a stone coffin, without a lid.

On attempting to unearth their "find" it crumbled to pieces, but among the *débris* was discovered a bag, full of something, which eventually turned out to be a mass of discoloured, but very perfectly preserved, silver coins of the Saxon period.

Among them were coins of Ælthelred and Alfred, 200 of Burgred of Mercia, and some coins of Louis le Debonnaire, and Charles le Chauve of France. Most of them found their way into the collection of Mr. John Evans F.R.S. Roman coins have also been found here.

the excavators found, at about two feet below the surface, a stone coffin without a lid

Coins of a more recent date, but of no less interest, have likewise been discovered here at different times. In the nineteenth volume of the *Archaeological Journal* for 1862 is the record of a discovery here, by Mr. W. Parker Hamond, of a French jeton, which was exhibited by him at a meeting of the Society; "on one side is Henry IV on horseback, on the other the arms of France and Navarre.

The counters struck at Nuremberg by Hans Krauwinckel and Wolfgang Laufer, for use in France, are numerous, and some of the types have an historical interest. Examples of the time of Henry IV are given by Snelling, J. de Fontenay, and other writers on jetons."

Roman Remains

A Roman road, which followed the lines of the ancient British Ermine Street, ran through the parish of Croydon. Gale, in his "Commentary" on the "Itinerary" of Antonius, says that the Roman road passed through Old Croydon from Woodcote to Streatham. From this circumstance is derived the name Streatham, "the home on the street." Hither, also, came a branch of the old Watling Street.

Naturally, we might expect to find a number of Roman remains in the parish, and we are not disappointed. Mr. Anderson says, "On the verge of the parish of Croydon, in 1871, the remains of a Roman villa were brought to light at Beddington.

"Other evidences of a former occupation of this neighbourhood by the Romans may be seen in the circumstance that, not long since, a small mutilated cup, or Roman vase, was dug up above the chalk-pit on Croham Farm. It was found at the back of the skull of a skeleton, duly laid on the chalk; there was no coin.

in 1871 the remains of a Roman villa were brought to light at Beddington

"A large, yellowish-red, coarse earthenware fragment of a neck and handles of an amphora was also recently dug up from a depth of about six feet - the last three being gravel - at the back of a cottage behind the waterworks, Surrey Street." Three coins - of Otho, Vespasian, and Hadrian - have also been picked up at different times in the parish.

The old town consists chiefly of one street, nearly a mile long, extending from the church to Haling. There appears to have been a town called Old Croydon, situated farther from London, towards Beddington, and some ruins of it were remaining in 1783.

Bits of Croydon Palace

1. West End of the Palace Chapel. 2. Buttresses of the North Side of the Chapel.
3. Porch to the Great Hall of the Palace, North Side. 4. From the South Side of the Great Hall.

Both Camden and Gale notice a tradition that there was anciently a royal palace southward of the present town, next Haling.

River Wandle

Through the spacious plain in which stand the palace and church, run various clear springs of water, which join to form the river Wandle. This river is mentioned by Pope in a well-known passage, where, speaking of the "brothers" of the Thames, he mentions "the blue transparent Vandalis." Camden remarks, "The Vandal is augmented by a small river from the east, which arises at Croydon formerly Craydiden, lying under the hills."

Croydon is singularly barren in historical reminiscences, apart from those associated with the palace, of which we shall speak presently, and the events relating to it are of little importance.

The Battle of Lewes

In 1264 a body of troops who had fought under the Earl of Leicester, consisting of Londoners, on returning home after the battle of Lewes, having taken up their quarters in this town, were attacked by the disbanded Royalists, who had formed the garrison of Tonbridge Castle, when many of them were killed, and their assailants obtained a great booty.

Stow's Chronicle

From "Stow's Chronicle" we learn that in 1286 "William Warren, son and heir of John Warren, Earle of Surrey, in a turneament at Croyden, was by the challenger intercepted, and cruelly slaine." From the same source, too, we learn that "in 1550, Grig, a poulterer, of Surrey, regarded among the people as a prophet, in curing divers diseases by words and prayers, and saying he would take no money, was, by commandment of the Earl of Warwick and others of the King's Council, set on a scaffold in the town of Croydon, with a paper on his breast, wherein were written his deceitful and hypocritical dealings. He was afterwards put in the pillory at Southwark during the Lady Day fair." Stow further tells us that in 1551 an earthquake was felt at Croydon, and several neighbouring places.

Grig was set on a scaffold in the town of Croydon with a paper on his breast wherein were written his deceitful and hypocritical dealings

Fuller, in his "Church History of Britain" (1656), after mentioning the Black Assizes at Oxford, in 1577, adds "The like chanced some four years since at Croydon, in Surrey, where a great depopulation happened at the assizes of persons of quality, and the two judges, Baron Yates and Baron Rigby, died a few days after."

The Plague

Lysons, in his "Environs," remarks that it does not appear by the register that there was any great mortality at Croydon about that time. The plague visited this town in 1603, and in that year and the next 158 persons died of it. The disease proved fatal to many people here also in 1625, 1626, 1631, 1665 and 1666. During the plague, in 1665, we are told several of the poorer classes buried their relations in the woods around the town.

The plague visited this town in 1603, and in that year and the next 158 persons died of it

Dr William Cleiver

In 1673 the parish was half ruined by a series of scandals, extending over thirteen years, alleged against the then vicar, Dr. William Cleiver, and the matter became so serious that the parishioners found themselves obliged to petition the Crown and the Legislature for his removal. It appears that the Doctor turned upon his assailants, and declared his intention to hold on his benefice, if only to spite the townspeople. In the end he resigned on a pension.

Violent Storms

From Steinman's "Croydon" we learn that "in 1728 so violent a storm of hail and rain, with thunder and lightning, fell at Croydon, as to strike the hailstones - which were from eight to ten inches round - some inches into the earth. The cattle were forced into the ditches and drowned, windows were shattered, and great damage done. Considerable damage in and near Croydon was also done by a storm of thunder and lightning in 1744."

The Parish Church of St. John the Baptist

The parish church is dedicated to St. John the Baptist - a dedication singularly appropriate, for it stood in a wildness, part of the great Forest of Surrey, which still survives in memory in the name of Norwood. Half a century ago the church stood on the bank of a rivulet, but this has been almost dried up by the subsequent drainage of the town.

Croydon from

uth-east (1885)

It is said that old people are still alive who remember minnows being caught quite close to the west end of the churchyard.

The surface of the ground all round the church and the palace has been gradually raised, the arches springing from a point only two or three feet from the present level.

The "Domesday Book" informs us that there was a church in Croydon at the time of the Conquest; and looking still further back, we find that a church must have stood here in the Anglo-Saxon era, for to the will of Byrhtric and Ælfwy, made in the year 960, a copy of which is printed in Lambard's "Perambulations of Kent," is affixed the name of Ælffie, priest of Croydon, as a witness.

Dr. Garrow, writing in 1818, describes the old church then existing as:

> "A very beautiful and stately Gothic structure, far surpassing every other church in the whole county of Surrey.

> "It has a lofty square tower of flint and stone, supported by well-proportioned buttresses at each angle; upon the top are four beautiful pinnacles, with a vane upon each. ...

> "This church is also distinguished by one of the finest organs in the kingdom, the exterior of which also corresponds very happily with the style of the architecture of the church. ...

> "The length of the nave is seventy-six feet, and that of the middle chancel fifty-four feet; the breadth of the church, with the aisles, is seventy-four feet. The nave is separated from the aisles by light clustered columns and Pointed arches, between which are several grotesque heads and ornaments. ...

> "The old font is at the west end of the south aisle, and appears, by its date and structure, to be coeval with the church. It is an octagon, with quarterfoils, in one of which is a lion's head in the centre; in two other adjoining ones are roses, the rest are concealed by pews."

The tower was repaired, and the buttresses disfigured by being encased in Roman cement in 1807-8.

Chantry Dedicated to St Mary the Virgin

There were formerly two chantries in this church, one dedicated to St. Mary the Virgin, the other to St. Nicholas. The first was founded by Sir Reginald de Cobham, of Starborough Castle, Surrey, about 1402. The incumbent was to pray for the souls of the said Sir Reginald, his wife, Joan, his children, and of all Christian people.

The founder vested the presentation to the preferment in the hands of twelve principal citizens of Croydon. The income of the chantry, derived from lands and tenements near Croydon, was £16.1s.2d. The chantry was dissolved under Edward VI, in 1547, a life pension of £6.13s.4d. in lieu thereof being granted to John Comporte, the last incumbent.

The Chantry Dedicated to St Nicholas

The other chantry, namely that dedicated to St. Nicholas, was founded "for the repose of the souls" of John Stafford, Bishop of Bath and Wells, and of William Oliver, vicar of Croydon.

The Weldon family is said to have possessed the patronage of this chantry, of which the total income was £14.14s. 6d. The last holder was Nicholas Sommer, to whom a pension of £6 13s. 4d. was granted at the dissolution of the monasteries.

"The mother-church of the parish," writes the author of the local handbook, "dates from the reign of Richard I, but not a stone of the original edifice now remains, except, perhaps, in the foundations, the building having twice been destroyed by fire.

"The venerable elm beside the gate, opposite the road leading to Waddon, is said to have been planted to mark the grave of a Knight Templar - slain probably in the skirmish of 1264."

The Rebuilt Church of 1867

The present church was reconstructed some few years ago on the site of the old structure, which was destroyed by fire in 1867.

It is a large and beautiful building of stone and flint, consisting of nave, aisles, and chancel, and a goodly proportioned tower at the western end of four stories surmounted by pinnacles at the angles.

It is in the Perpendicular style, and some of the windows are enriched with painted glass, that at the east end of the chancel being particularly fine.

The venerable elm beside the gate, opposite the road leading to Waddon, is said to have been planted to mark the grave of a Knight Templar slain probably in the skirmish of 1264

Sir Gilbert Scott restored the church mainly on the old lines

The nave is separated from the aisles by arcades of six arches, and has an oak roof of rich design; the chancel has a panelled roof with massive moulded ribs, at the springing of which are figures of angels holding musical instruments: the seats in the chancel are most elaborately and beautifully carved; there is an alabaster reredos and stone sedile on the south side.

The situation of the church, together with its surroundings, is very pleasing, the churchyard being well planted with evergreens, and containing some noble trees, the foliage of which contrasts strikingly with the red brick walls and other remains of the old palace adjacent.

The ancient walls of the Norman church - or, at all events, large portions of them - are still there, encased, within and without, by the new facings added by Sir Gilbert Scott.

The restoration of the church brought to light several curious objects, among others a holy-water stoup, inside the south door, and the sills of several windows, the existance of which had been quite forgotten.

Sir Gilbert Scott restored the church mainly on the old lines, though he lengthened the fabric by eighteen feet, and raised the clerestory windows and the roof. The work was carried out at a cost of £28,000. A new peal of eight bells, with a carillon machine playing fourteen tunes, by Messrs. Gillett, Bland, & Co., of this town, was hung in the western tower, and a new and magnificent organ, by Mr. A. G. Hill, was erected, in the place of the one that had been destroyed.

Amongst those buried in the old church are John Singleton Copley, R.A. (the father of Lord Lyndhurst), and Cottingham, the architect. The monument of the latter, by Flaxman, was destroyed in the fire.

Archbishops of Canterbury

Archbishops Wake, Herring, and Potter, all lie buried in the chapel adjoining the southern side of the chancel, but their monuments have perished, though tablets of brass have been newly inserted in the walls to record their names.

Here, too, are buried Archbishops Whitgift, Wake, Grindal, and Sheldon. Three out of the four were buried under handsome monuments. The monuments of Grindal, Whitgift, and Sheldon, were destroyed in the fire of 1867, but the two latter were not past repair, and that of Whitgift has been duly restored.

A corner of Croydon Palace

It would be a graceful act if the University of Cambridge, with which Sheldon was connected as a benefactor, would apply the same process to his monument. The iron railings saved the marble from utter destruction, though the fire cracked and broke it, and destroyed the colours.

Archbishop Grindal

In the middle of the chancel, on a sarcophagus within an arched recess, the entablature of which was supported by Corinthian columns, lay the painted effigy of Archbishop Grindal in his scarlet robes.

Surmounting the entablature were three armorial shields, bearing respectively the arms of the sees of York, Canterbury, and London. The Archbishop died in 1583.

Archbishop Sheldon

The monument to the memory of Archbishop Sheldon was of very beautiful design and exquisite workmanship. It stood in St. Nicholas' Chantry, and bore upon it the recumbent effigy of the prelate in his archiepiscopal robes and mitre. The altartomb, in which the Archbishop appeared to repose, was of black marble. Its panels were enriched by some finely-carved osteology.

The figure itself was of statuary marble, beautifully sculptured; the left hand sustained the head, in the right was a crozier. Above the figure was an inscription, surmounted by a cherubim supporting an armorial shield. This monument was designed by Joseph Latham, the City mason, and entirely executed by him and his English workmen. The Archbishop died at Croydon in 1677.

Archbishop Whitgift

The tomb of Archbishop Whitgift greatly resembles that of Archbishop Grindal, it being a sarcophagus supported by Corinthian columns of black marble. It is surmounted by the recumbent effigy of the prelate in sable robes, with his hands joined as in prayer; and its three shields bear respectively the arms of the see of Canterbury and Worcester and the deanery of Lincoln.

On the panels of the sarcophagus are the armorial bearings of the see of Lincoln, and of the colleges of Trinity, Pembroke, and Peterhouse, at Cambridge. Whitgift died in 1604; his funeral was solemnised in a manner suitable to the splendour in which he had lived.

"The tombs of Archbishops Grindal, Whitgift, and other Archbishops," writes Evelyn, in his "Diary," under date of August 13, 1700, "are fine and venerable, but none comparable to that of the late Archbishop Sheldon, which being all of white marble and of a stately ordnance and carvings, far surpass'd the rest, and I judge could not cost less than 7 or 8 hundred pounds."

Monuments in the Old Church

The old church contained many interesting monuments and epitaphs, of which we may mention one or two conspicuous for quaintness and unconscious humour. For instance, the following magnificent effort of some neglected son of Apollo:-

"Heare lies buried the corps
Of Maister Henry Mill,
Citezen and grocer of
London famous cittie.

Alderman, and somtyme shreve,
A man of prudent skill,
Charitable to the poore,
And alwaies full of pittie,
Whose soul we hope doth rest in
Blise, wheare joy doth still abounde,
Though bodie his full depe do lie
In earth here, under grounde."

Here, too, were several monuments to the Herons, Whitgifts, Greshams, Phippses, Scudamores, Mortons, Wyvills, Bainbridges, Pennymans, Champions, and Brigstocks.

It would seem as if good husbands and wives were rare at Croydon; at all events, a marble monument on the north wall of the old church, to the memory of John and Elizabeth Parker, who died in 1706 and 1730 respectively, bore this laudatory inscription:-

"This pair, whilst they lived together, were a pattern for conjugal behaviour; he a careful, indulgent husband, she a tender, engaging wife; he active in business, punctual to his word, kind to his family, generous to his friends, but charitable to all; possessed of every social virtue. During her widowhood she carefully and virtuously educated five children, who survived her. She was an excellent economist, modest without affectation, religious without superstition, and in every action behaved with uncommon candour and steadiness."

The following curious epitaph was inscribed on a vault near the north entrance of the churchyard, but Steinman, in his "History of Croydon" (1833), states it to be "now lost" :-

"Mr. William Burnet. Born January 29th 1685.
Died October 29th 1760.

"WHAT IS MAN?"

To-day he's dust in gold and silver bright,
Wrapt in a shroud before to-morrow night;
To-day he's feasting on delicious food,
To-morrow nothing eat can do him good;
To-day he's nice, and scorns to feed on crumbs,
In a few days himself a dish for worms;
To-day he's honoured, and in great esteem,
To-morrow not a beggar values him;
To-day he rises from a velvet bed,
To-morrow lies in one that's rapt in lead;
To-day his house, though large, he thinks too small,
To-morrow can command no house at all;
To-day has twenty servants at his gate,
To-morrow scarcely one will deign to wait;
To-day perfumed, and sweet as is the rose,
To-morrow, stinks in everybody's nose;
To-day he's grand, majestic, all delight,
Ghastly and pale before to-morrow night.

"Now, when you've wrote and said whate'er you can,
This is the best that you can say of MAN."

In 1845-6 some curious frescoes were accidentally discovered on the walls of the old church, of which the following particulars are recorded in the *Archaeological Journal* for 1846 :-

"The Rev. Henry Lindsay, Vicar of Croydon, expressed his wish that some member of the committee should examine the curious mural painting, which has been recently discovered in the church of Croydon, previously to its being concealed again from view, in consequence of the decision of the churchwardens that the whole shall shortly be coloured over.

"The subject is St. Christopher: a little apart from the principal figure are portraits of a king and queen, in fair preservation. Mr. Lindsay supposes that they represent Edward III and Queen Philippa. There are also traces of an inscription."

April 23rd:

"Dr. Bromet exhibited drawings of the distemper painting lately discovered in Croydon Church, Surrey. It represents St. Christopher, and is painted on the south wall, opposite to the north door."

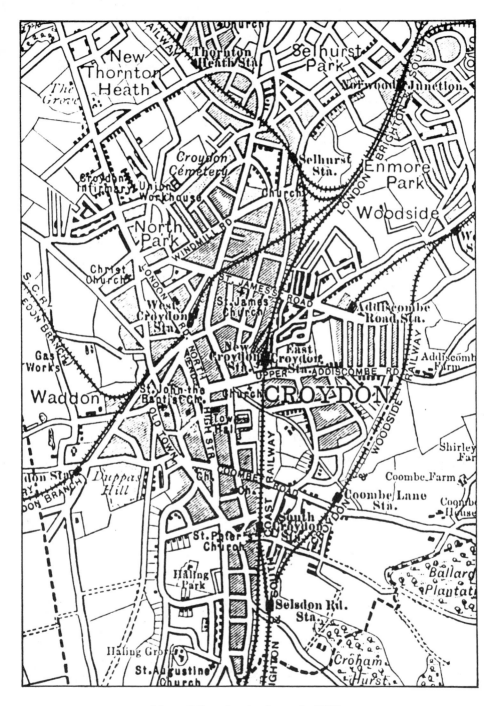

Map of Croydon in the early 1880s

June 23rd:

> "Dr. Bromet exhibited a drawing by M. G. J. L. Noble, and tracings taken by himself from some portions of the distemper painting recently discovered in Croydon Church, accompanied by the following observations:-

> "On the south wall, and opposite to the north door of Croydon Church, is a colossal figure of St. Christopher, of which the general design is so grand and elegant, that I regret much to report that its ornamental details are not easily discernable, and also that nothing more of the Christ than the feet is now visible; the legs of St. Christopher also are hidden buy some panelling.

> "The drapery of this figure is a purplish coloured tunic and a green cloak, and the folds of both are artistically disposed. In his hands he bears a knotted staff, which, though green, is not in that sprouting state occasionally seen. ...

> "On the left of the saint, though not relating to any legend concerning him that I can find, is a semi-circularly-arched and portcullised embattled gateway, over which, at a quadrangular window in a lofty tower, seemingly of brick with stone dressings, are the figures of a king and queen.

> "The king has a flowing grey beard, and is habited in a purplish tunic, with an ermine collar and red cloak. The queen is much younger, with auburn hair, and is in a purplish robe, lined with red."

These frescoes were destroyed by the fire, as also were the bells in the western tower. The first of these bells was thus inscribed :-

> "My voice I will raise,
> And sound my subscribers' praise
> At proper times.
> Thomas Lster made me, 1738."

The king has a flowing grey beard, and is habited in a purplish tunic, with an ermine collar and red cloak

Croydon seems to have been a healthy place, for we find recorded the deaths of five centenarians, of whom one, Margaret Ford, reached the age of 105 years

Francis Tyrrell, citizen and grocer of London, who died in 1600, was commemorated on his brass in the church, as having given to the parish £200 to build a new market-house, and £40 to beautify the church and to make a "Sainte's bell."

The Parish Registers

The registers of Croydon parish commenced in 1538, when Thomas Cromwell, Vicar-General, issued an order that parish registers should be kept throughout the kingdom. Croydon seems to have been a healthy place, for we find recorded the deaths of five centenarians, of whom one, Margaret Ford, reached the age of 105 years.

Among the entries of burials we find the names of Whitgift, "Gilbert Sheldon," Dr. Wake, Dr. Potter, and Dr. Herring, Archbishops of Canterbury, and "My Lady Scudamore," the aunt of the poet Edmund Waller.

Bishops Consecrated at Croydon Church

The following bishops were consecrated in Croydon Church :-

1534 (April 19th) - By Archbishop Cranmer, Thomas Goodrich, D.D., Bishop of Ely, and John Capon, alias Salcot, LL.D., late Abbot of Hide, Bishop of Bangor.

1541 (September 25th) - By the same archbishop: John Wakeman, last Abbot of Tewkesbury, and first Bishop of Gloucester.

1551 (August 30th) - By the same archbishop: John Scory, D.D., Bishop of Rochester, and Miles Coverdale, Bishop of Exeter.

1591 (August 29th) - by Archbishop Whitgift: Gervase Babington, D.D., Bishop of Llandaff.

1612 (September 20th) - By Archbishop Abbott, assisted by John (King), Bishop of London: Richard (Neile), Bishop of Lichfield and Coventry, and John (Buckeridge), Bishop of Rochester, Miles Smith, D.D., Bishop of Gloucester.

In the year 1417 the sacred edifice was polluted by bloodshed

This church appears to have been singularly unfortunate in its career. In the year 1417 the sacred edifice was polluted by bloodshed - possibly accidentally, or in some popular affray, for the country at that date was at peace. At all events we find Archbishop Chicheley, in the February of that year, issuing a commission to another ecclesiastic to "reconcile" the church and churchyard.

During the fanatical outbreak of the Great Rebellion, the notorious "Will Dowsing," the iconoclast of the Eastern Counties, found his counterpart at Croydon; for Aubrey tells us in his "Antiquities of Surrey,"* that "one Bleese was hired, for half-a-crown a day, to break the painted windows, which were formerly fine."

On the 25th of December, 1639, a violent storm of wind blew down one of the pinnacles of the steeple, which fell upon the roof, and did great damage; and in 1744 the church was considerably damaged by lightning.

Fires at the Church

On the 11th March, 1734-5, between two and three o'clock in the afternoon, as the parish register informs us, "a fire was discovered in the roof of the middle chancel, which is supposed to have been caused by some embers carelessly left there by the plumbers. It was soon extinguished, and the damage done did not exceed £50."

Finally, in the evening of the 5th of January, 1867, as stated above, this fine old church was destroyed by fire, nothing but the bare walls being left standing.

Dr William Cleiver

A singular story is told in Captain Smith's "Lives of Highwaymen," respecting Dr. William Cleiver, or Clewer, who held the vicarage of Croydon in the seventeenth century. He appears to have been collated by Archbishop Juxon in 1660, at the recommendation of Charles II, who had been imposed upon with regard to his character.

"Dr. Cleiver," remarks Steinman, "was notorious for his singular love of litigation, unparalleled extortions, and criminal and disgraceful conduct, which eventually caused his ejectment from this benefice in 1684.

* See "Greater London" Volume II page 30.

Croydon Church Tower in 1785

He was a great persecutor of the Royalists during the Commonwealth

"He was a great persecutor of the Royalists during the Commonwealth; and enjoyed the sequestered living of Ashton, Northamptonshire, to which he was appointed in 1645, being at that time, according to Walker, scarce eighteen, 'of a very ill life, and very troublesome to his neighbours.' "* He died in 1702, and was buried at St. Bride's, Fleet Street, in the register of which church he is styled "Parson of Croydon."

The following is the story above referred to :-

"O'Bryan, meeting with Dr. Cleiver the parson of Croydon (*try'd once and burnt in the hand at the Old Bailey for stealing a silver cup*), coming along the road from Acton, he demanded his money; but the reverend doctor having not a farthing about him, O'Bryan was for taking his gown. At this our divine was much dissatisfied; but, perceiving the enemy would plunder him quoth he, 'Pray, sir, let me have a chance for my gown;' so, pulling a pack of cards out of his pocket, he farther said, 'We'll have, if you please, one game of all fours for it, and if you win it take it and wear it.' This challenge was readily accepted by the foot-pad, but being more cunning than his antagonist at slipping and palming the cards, he won the game, and the doctor went contentedly home without his canonicals."

The Parsonage

The parsonage formerly stood at the south-west corner of the churchyard, opposite to a spot now marked by a drinking fountain; beside it bubbled a small brook, here broadened into a pond, where boys caught gudgeon, and occasionally even trout. The vicarage garden was added to the churchyard, which the old garden shrubs still adorn. The vicarage house was rebuilt by Archbishop Wake in 1730; but it appears that there was a vicarage house here as far back as the reign of Edward III.

Whilst the patronage of the vicarage remained with the archbishop, the rectory manor, after the Reformation, passed into lay hands. It belonged in turn to the families of the Herons, the St. Johns, and the Walsinghams; and it appears to have been conveyed by the Hon. Robert Boyle Walsingham, in the year 1770, to Anthony Browne, Lord Montagu, of Cowdray Park, in Sussex, who came to his death by drowning at the Falls of Schaffhausen, on the Rhine.

* Walker's "List of the Ejected Clergy" Part II page 402

Also available
in this series

Walford's History of
Croydon Palace

Walford's History of
The Whitgift Hospital
and Other Croydon Charities

Walford's History of
Croydon Town and Suburbs

LOCAL HISTORY REPRINTS

Local History Reprints is a non-profit making publisher that reprints antiquarian, Victorian, Edwardian and other local history publications that are now out of print and unavailable.

It specialises in material of interest to the local and family historian, or those who wish to discover more about the area in which they live, with the aim of promoting a greater awareness of a locality's heritage and encouraging research into its past.

Contemporary local histories are also published.

Publications available cover the following areas:

**ADDINGTON
BALHAM
BATTERSEA
CARSHALTON
CLAPHAM
CROYDON
CRYSTAL PALACE
MERTON
MITCHAM
PUTNEY
STREATHAM
SUTTON
TOOTING
WANDSWORTH
WIMBLEDON**

For details concerning the full range of publications available please forward a stamped addressed envelope to the undermentioned address.

ISBN 1 85699 028 1

LOCAL HISTORY REPRINTS

316 GREEN LANE, STREATHAM, LONDON SW16 3AS